Double Trouble Vol. II – Jose & James

I ask her why she is in this bar having a drink with me.
She says she's always been in this bar drinking with me.

(excerpt from poem "Carson McCullers")

**Other Collaborations
by Matthew Jose and Candice James**

Double Trouble Volume I - poems from the edge
Silver Bow Publishing 2019

Double Trouble Vol. II

Deviate the Levitate

By

**Matthew Jose
&
Candice James**

720 Sixth Street, Unit #5,
New Westminster, BC Canada
V3L3C5

Title: Double Trouble Vol. II deviate the levitate
Authors: Matthew Jose and Candice James
Publisher: Silver Bow Publishing
Cover Art/Design: "Of One Blood They Enter" painting by Candice James:
Layout and editing: Candice James

All rights reserved including the right to reproduce or translate this book or any portions thereof, in any form without the permission of the publisher. Except for the use of short passages for review purposes, no part of this book may be reproduced, in part or in whole, or transmitted in any form or by any means, electronically or mechanically, including photocopying, recording, or any information or storage retrieval system without prior permission in writing from the publisher or a license from the Canadian Copyright Collective Agency (Access Copyright). Copyright to all individual poems remains with the author.
© Silver Bow Publishing 2021

97817740301650 Print
97817740301667 epub

Library and Archives Canada Cataloguing in Publication

Title: Double trouble. Vol. II : deviate the levitate / by Matthew Jose & Candice James.
Other titles: Deviate the levitate
Names: Jose, Matthew, 1976- author. | James, Candice, 1948- author.
Identifiers: Canadiana (print) 20210169559 | Canadiana (ebook) 20210169575 | ISBN 9781774031650
   (softcover) | ISBN 9781774031667 (Kindle)
Classification: LCC PS3610.O75 D69 2021 | DDC 811/.6—dc23

To all the poets who persevere
and the eclectic audience
that appreciates their lore

~ Matthew Jose & Candice James

Contents

Clawfoot Tub and the Bearded Barbarian ... 9
Luvven It ... 11
A Peculiar Tale of Chess (aka Dedeeron and Squatty) ... 13
Carson McCullers (aka the Sonnie Boy enigma) ... 15
The Vibe ... 17
Delicious Adocious ... 19
Ashes and the Interview ... 20
The Answer to All That ... 22
Essence of Al Purdy ... 24
From Poetry to Zen and Back ... 26
Who Is Grady Lewis Anyway? ... 28
Disney Out-Takes ... 29
To Sup of the Universal Language ... 31
Innocent Bystanders ... 34
Do You Know the Type? ... 36
Look and See ... 38
Realization Departed ... 39
Key to the Secret   .40
In Between the Yawning and the Yawning ... 42
The Finest of Lines ... 44
Deviate the Levitate ... 47
Don't Just Don't ... 49
Extraordinary, Perhaps, Probably ... 51
Pardon Me, Excuse Me, Allow Me ... 52
Human Supposition ... 54
But Not For Me ... 55
Old Irish, Me and My Kazoo ... 56
The Universe Will ... 58
What Happens is This ... 60
On Becoming Ricky Nelson ... 63
Degrees ... 64
Him Not Hem ... 65
A – maze – ing ... 66
The Search Never Ends ... 67
Random Moon Boy ... 69
Boondoggle Boggle in the Boondocks ... 70
Psychosomatic Fallacies ... 72

Finicky Wicket ... 75
One Moment to Another ... 78
Waiting ... 79
Fruit of the Fodder ... 80
Signals ... 82

Authors' Profile ... 84

Clawfoot Tub and the Bearded Barbarian

A joke is never as good when it has to be explained
but try telling that to a bearded barbarian
with fierce eyes who thinks he's a real cut up.
I better not tell him he's a fake paper cut-out doll
and a wanna-be dinner winner.

The two of us were the last two
waiting to take the stage at an open mic
and as I was about to walk out and wow the crowd
he tapped me on the shoulder, a tad roughly too,
and asked if I minded if he went on before me.

I wasn't sure how I felt, as a poet,
if I was to have to follow a comedian to the stage
but I also wasn't sure how I felt about a lot of things
so I turned around and said to him,
"Sure funny man, have at it."

I missed the first half of his probably inglorious set
because I was so deep into my own glorious head.
Something had been bothering me all day;
for the life of me I couldn't remember
if the bath water spins down the drain
in a clockwise or counter clockwise motion
as it empties out of my clawfoot tub.

Thinking about this made me wonder about clubfeet.
I wondered what they looked like...
I hadn't seen a clubfoot, ever.
I wondered if maybe the inventor of the clawfoot tub
was an unimaginative guy with a clubfoot
who couldn't think of a name for his tub,
so as he was taking his sock off
and scratching his foot, he said to himself ....
'I know. I'll call it a Clawfoot tub!'

Probably not, but stranger things have happened
in my world of oddities, that's for sure.

Still stuck grading the motion of bathwater
as it runs its marathon race to the drain:
clockwise or counter-clockwise?
upside-down or down-side up?
All I know is that last bit of bath water
always leaves with a strangled gush and gurgle
like a choking man drowning in his own bullshit.

This brings me back to the bearded barbarian
who pushed his way in front of me at the open-mic,
because it was all about him and HE had to be first.
He just finished-up his angst amateur set
to the deafening quiet of muted applause.
I guess the funny man wasn't so funny after all.
What a joke!

I walk out on-stage to the roar of the crowd
and in the beta-cam part of my cinemascope mind
I see the bearded barbarian miniaturizing
and screaming as he slides down the drain
of my dangerous, dastardly clawfoot tub.

I grab onto the mic.
I close my eyes,
close the bathroom door in my mind.

I take a deep breath ...
and the performance begins.

Luvven It

I'd been so busy trying to invent explanations
I was starting to miss the show. The real deal.
But it wasn't altogether my fault, you see,
she's the one who kept asking me who I thought I was.
How on earth am I supposed to know who I am?

I tried to explain what it's like.
I can be a different version of myself each day.
Sometimes I eat and then I dress.
And sometimes I dress and then I eat.
There's no set pattern to my actions
and there's def no set pattern to me.

That wasn't enough for her though.
She said she needed consistency.
I told her only a fool expects consistency.
Insert note to self here...never imply foolhardiness
when speaking to a woman. She went quiet
and I used the silent space to head into my head.

I started thinking about puppets and plasticine
and the consistency of Pudding-Cake Man...
He was a puppet I made out of plasticine as a kid,
but he was a big, humongous disappointment,
I couldn't attach strings to make him a puppet
and he was too wobbly to be a stand up guy.

Then I thought about the word 'foolhardiness'.
I took out the fool and the ness and was left with hardi.
I exchanged the "i" for a "y" to make it a surname ... Hardy.
That set me to wondering why nobody with that last name
ever had a first name like "fool" or "goof" or "clown".

Then I thought ... what if the first name was "Hardy"?
Then we could do a Jackie Gleason roundabout of Harhar.
Hardy Harhar. I like that.
Or if you were at a café having fish and chips

and the condiments always arrive late
you could be saucy and call the café the Tardy Tartar.
But I digress. Let's get back to being foolhardy.

If my first name was Fool and my last name Hardy
and she changed her surname "It" her first name to "Luvven,
we'd be a match made in heaven
especially when making an entrance at posh cocktail parties
like Buckingham Palace, the Presidential ball etc.
"Announcing the Duke of Nonsense, Fool Hardy
and his loving partner, the Duchess, "Luvven It.
And all through the reception we'd be introduced
time and time again "Fool Hardy and Luvven It"

If we ever have kids our first born will be named
Riddick U. Luss Hardy.

My predilection with the far out and the fantastic
is and always has been unwavering
through all things, real and unreal.
So, how can she say I'm inconsistent?
I am the close-up epitome of a far man
just playin' the hand he's been dealt
Is that okay with you Vonie Flummerfelt?
If not, just change your name to something simple.
Try Luvven It.

A Peculiar Tale of Chess
(aka Dedeeron and Squatty)

A late move can be a great move
and the last move is often the best move.
But I rarely win at chess.
I love to play and all, but it just isn't my strong suit.
I'm a shaker not a mover ... a groover not a quaker.

I learned early on
no matter which direction you long to travel in
you're going to need wind in the sails
regardless of your best laid plans or strategy.
On the high seas of life ... without a friendly wind,
you just ain't goin' nowhere buds.

And I found out in my younger Polo days
it ain't the wood or the size of the mallet,
it's the strength in the arm and the twist of the wrist
regardless of the proximity of the ball.
Same way with golf, really.
It's keeping your eye on the ball and choosing the right iron.

Where were we?
Oh yes, the chess match.
Yeah, so this pre-teen girl,
who couldn't have been older than 12,
beat me in 6 moves once.
She told me it was the fastest she
had ever been able to beat someone.

Was I supposed to stand up and clap and cheer?
Celebrate that crowning achievement with her?
Never one to choke down the soured milk in my glass,
I stood ever so graciously and shook her hand
and offered a mighty, yet hollow, congratulations
then decided to head westward ho, sans wagon, on foot
into the more densely forested part of the park.
This is where the story gets peculiar...

I overheard whispers, high pitched whispers
coming from behind a sparsely clothed Juniper bush.
I edged closer, not wanting to eavesdrop
but somehow feeling compelled to do so.

It was a gathering of miniature chess players flapping their gums.
The short squat one with turquoise skin was palavering on …
"How did she do it? Dedeeron is not that smart.
How did she make herself grow larger and change her skin colour?"
The others didn't seem too interested in what Squatty was saying.
One threw an apple core at him shouting "Shaddup Squatty"
He continued rambling on. "And to think she took all our moves
and beat that goofy guy in 6 moves. That's cheating!
I mean, for Gugaka's sake, she was playing with an Earthling
who doesn't know she has every chess move ever made
immediately accessible by just touching the end of her nose.
Hell he doesn't know the difference
between his arsehole and a hole in the ground.
That poor sucker didn't have a chance."

That was all I needed to hear.
I saw her touch her nose exactly 6 times!
I rushed back to tell the judges
what a goddamned fake cheater she was,
but, who'd believe me? I would find it hard to believe me.
She looked so young and sweet and innocent and perfect,
like nothing could rankle her at all.

Squatty was wrong. Dedeeron was smart. really smart.
He couldn't change his size or his skin colour like she could,
but Squatty was also very right too.
I didn't have a chance then, and I didn't have a chance now.
Winning and exposition mix like oil and water. They don't.

As I reached the judges table, I faltered for a moment,
decided to save my breath, and my rep too,
so I just smiled and just kept on a walkin' …
possibly even to New Orleans.

Carson McCullers
(and the Sonnie Boy enigma)

As time swoons and sways backwards
the expression of the melody becomes clearer.
Damn, I wish I could have had a drink
with the famous Grand Shaman of Maman,
Carson McCullers the great soothsayer of my dreams.
I'd like to think that when we first met
there would have been an acknowledging eye moment
followed by a kind of deep scary silence.
But a good one, you know?

And that would be followed by a discussion
about beef versus smoked salmon in sandwich form
as far as which is better or even more educational.
And then of course followed by that drink.
Some hot Long Island Tea and top of the mark sherry
followed by an in-depth discussion
as far as which is better or even more musical.
Her drink would be in a thermos with the Star Trek emblem
and mine would be in a fancy crystal cordial glass, of course.
And she would spend the first ten minutes of our conversation
explaining to me why she calls her drink Sonnie Boy.

Kazoom Bada Boom. Wowzers.
Thunder and lightning, Mind blast and sonic zap.
Time warped, then shifted and opened up
and now she is sitting right here in front of me
sipping her drink and talking to me as if I was always there.
She said she is amazed that I spelled Sonnie Boy right..
Says most people spell it Sonny Boy or Sunny Boy.
Says most drinkers are illiterate. Says she's never wrong.
She leaves it at that and I am no the wiser
regarding the name Sonnie Boy and what it means to her.
She doesn't give me a clue as to why she calls it Sonnie Boy.
I decide to leave it alone and switch the convo up.
I ask her why she is in this bar having a drink with me.
She says she's always been in this bar drinking with me.

Double Trouble Vol. II – Jose & James

I motion the waiter over and ask for a smoked salmon sandwich.
She orders a Little Dipper beef dip, easy on the salt.
Says she's already had too much in her earlier Jose Cuervos.
Says she doesn't want her face to puff up like a Puffer Fish.
Has to keep her image, you know, she's a fashion fashionista.

While we are deep in conversation the sandwiches arrive.
We keep talking, immersed in convo, eyes locked on each other,
while we absentmindedly pick up the sandwich on our right.
We are so engrossed in each other, the convo and the drink
that we don't notice we have each other's sandwich.
I think it's because we have each other's eyes
which are the mirrors of the soul, so they say,
and when I say "so they say"
I mean the followers of the absentee Sonnie Boy.

We drink and we talk and we talk and we drink
and the time just slip slides away in a gloss
on a skating rink of quantum particles ...
and as I take my last sip and put my glass down
I'm back in the same old bar with me, myself and I.

It's then that I realize we are all one ...
Me, myself and I and ... Carson McCullers.

The Vibe

I've known love.
I've showed love.
I've grown love.
I've feigned love.
I've laughed because of love.
I've cried because of love.

All this because "love is the answer"
used to ring loudly around the area
I used to live in.
And it's not, not true.
It's just not true, true.
As in always and forever.

I wanted to believe all this.
And still do on some level at certain times.
But even at those certain times,
it can't be forced.
I guess that's what I'm trying to say.

I've seen a bunch of mid-life crisis events.
And sure, one thing that was missing
in each of the equations was love.
I can't deny that.

I've seen plenty of families fall apart.
And again, love was the missing link.

Wait, maybe there is something to this love thing.
But that word. Love. Maybe that's the problem.
It doesn't mean the same thing to everybody.

Humans throw that word around
like it's not the power of the universe.
Humans use that word
when talking about ice cream for Christ's sake.
Ok Ok Ok. That must be it.

The word needs to be replaced by a vibration.
But how would we talk about it then?
That's the point mebbee...
Mebbee love isn't meant to be said.
Mebbee it's just meant to be:
Felt.
Shown.
Grown.
But never feigned.

Here's what I believe
and you can take it to heart like a lover
or stomp on it like a fool.

I believe:
The feeling is the music.
The eyes are the tell.
The heart is the beat.

The music, the tell and the beat
all toning together into the vibration.

Some call it love ...
I call it 'the vibe'.

Delicious — Adocious

By the time I got there,
there was only one flower left.
So I grabbed it right at the spot
where the stem and ground
were one and the same.

I said hello then carefully placed the flower
behind her right ear
and placed my hand on her spine
as her lips touched mine.

Our lips spontaneously began to melt
and took on the viscosity
and characteristics of fondue.

Cheese or chocolate you ask?
Kind of a combination of both.
Now, I know that sounds gross.
Chocolate covered cheese?
Cheese covered chocolate?
Yes. Just like that.
And it was delicious somehow.

She was delicious. I was delicious.
I was Jim and she was Phyllis
We were 'mmmm ... delicious'.
I was Dick and she was Julie
just 'pop, pop poppins' along
when we both became that
which we never imagined becoming ...
Supercalifragilisticexpialadocious.

Ashes and the Interview

What a freezing cold night to be raking in all these hot ashes.
Somewhere along the way the path must have vanished.
But then I remember what the yogi in India told me,
"You only have one place to be. It's here. Now."
He told me that and also in the same breath said,
"For the life of me I can never figure out
which way a stream moves, but I know for sure
it flows with quite a strength after a rainfall.
And it's everchanging as with the changing winds."
I realized then that there are things that never remain the same.
Just remembering that was enough.
So I raked up all the ashes in front of me
and also a few piles scattered about
that must have changed direction
that weren't even on my account.
They just didn't belong, but then, sometimes ...
I just don't belong, so I raked them up anyway
out of pity, so they wouldn't feel lost and lone.
Like the actual outcasts they really were.

The wind knows their names, but it won't speak them
The rain knows their water levels but won't spill them out.
The sun knows their ability to sparkle or not
The moon knows the secrets they whisper to the night
and the stars know they're just dead or dying fire babies.
The ashes, alert or semi-comatose are oblivious to all this stuff.
They just keep scattering around in a bizarre 5 step
to the paranoid symphony orchestra only they hear.
The trumpet player never fails to play a few wrong notes
and the hippy happy drummer misses a whack of beats
hence these haphazard out of step outcast ashes
 end up dancing with my well-rehearsed ashes
and wreaking havoc on all that is musically holy.
Ashes to ashes. Dust to dust
Is not spoken of the unwelcome cacophony.
It just goes on and on and on and on ...
An interviewer once asked me about these hot ashes

I was always raking up on freezing cold nights.
I told him they were bits and pieces of unfinished poem
ones that I still may have a chance of resurrecting,
He asked me if these poems
were born out of real life experiences.
I told him I wasn't necessarily a believer in real life
so I didn't know how to answer the question.
So next he asked where the ideas came from.
I told him ideas always comes forward in one form or another
and I was just glad the ideas had formed words
and found a home with my semi-comatose ashes.
These living words could breathe life into my half-dead ashes
that were aching to come out of stasis and be poems again
Really. That's the gift. That's the blessing.
New ideas and life coalescing with old ashes and death
to become something never-ending and beautiful.
Something that will live forever throughout time.
And, speaking of time – that elusive old devil...
I could see he was growing weary of my voice,
yawning and fidgeting around in his chair,
nevertheless, I continued on before he could interrupt ...
I didn't want any more question once I stopped talking.
I told him I went through a disturbing phase
where I would set all sorts of random alarms
on all the clocks throughout my house.
And they would just keep going off all day long.
And I loved that. The strict strange music of time.

Then, I stopped talking.
Seconds stretched into minutes.
He didn't ask me any more questions after that.
And the silence was golden.

The Answer to All That

It was something in the nature of a hoax.
A fraud of a very different flavor, for sure.
But the same veiled deception shawled over
and lined the domains of the experiences.
A couple frothy pints and a couple full-on puffs
made it so obvious that it was impossible to see.
For most.
But not for me.
Oh no, no, no.

I've always known it was the smaller fish milling about
that were the real catch. The fisherman's caviar.
I know it's the bigger fish that get all the attention from the deep fryers,
but the smaller ones are where the real nutrients reside.

Anyway. In my lifetime I've seen men become women
and women become men.
I've seen poor people become rich
and rich people become poor.
I've seen humans of all sorts, of all shades and colors
hate and kill other humans of all sorts, of all shades and colors
for all sorts of black, beige and white reasons.

I would never dare to say I've seen it all
because I know we aren't even close to that yet.
But I've certainly seen some things in my days.
And no matter what I see, or don't see,
I'm always left with the same thoughts / questions:
Why weren't we created with arms just a little longer
so as to avoid the failed gymnastics of trying to reach
that unreachable and damnable spot on the back
where the itches always seem to manifest most often?
Why aren't our heads totally flexible and rotational
so we can see what's behind us in one quick neck snap?
And why don't we have 4 sets of eyes. 2 in front. 2 in back
that way we would have unimpeded peripheral vision,

and chances of becoming totally blind would virtually be nil.
And why don't we have double of everything
in the realm of soft tissue and organs: heart in particular.
Like the song says "You've Gotta Have Heart"
We can't live without a heart, so why did we only get one??

I think I have the answer to all that ...

We are all children of God,
and he probably misses us,
so he only gives us a short tenure of time
away from him.
Like any father, he looks in on his kids
from time to time,
but doesn't interfere with our progress
unless necessary.

Sometimes he brings us home early.
Sometimes he just needs a bloody good rest from us.
And sadly, some of us never see home or Dad again.

So, God bless the orphans ...
may they one day be taken back home
or at least adopted
by some universal fishers of men.

Essence of Al Purdy

What a wonderful sleep I just had.
And the dream I had within it was ...
more like an awakening than a dream.

It started with the vision of a pristine, white wash basin
and as I got closer look, I could see it wasn't water inside it.
It was filled with a glowing deep purple liquid,
deeper than the deepest shade one could ever imagine.
The basin was set against an enchanted
but mostly forgotten background motif from yesteryear.

As I leaned over to smell the juicy goodness,
I heard a voice from behind me say
"It's different from the kind you will find in Japan."
I turned to see Al Purdy, standing there, alive and well,
big-assed stogie in the left corner of his mouth,
hair flowing wild and free ... like the man and his poetry.

I asked him if he knew what was in the basin.
He answered with a sneer and a snort and said,
"Know what's in it? I made what's in it kid!
I made it from my blood, sweat and tears.
My gut rumbles, constipation and headaches.
My misconceptions and my failings.
My glories and my moments of grandeur,
no matter how short-lived or fleeting.
I made it from ME. I call it Essence of Al Purdy.
And let me tell you, with a very certain clarity,
birthing a long awaited and hard-fought crap
is more like beginning and finishing a poem
than anyone, other than a true poet,
could ever imagine, even in their wildest dreams.

Because he shared this very personal info with me,
I thought I was now one of his inner circle.
A comrade in paper, words and thought.
So, I asked him if I could partake of the majestic purple.

He said "I bet you think it's homemade Saki, right? Well it isn't.
It's Thoughti and Braini, and Hearti of Purdy
and it will make anyone but Al Purdy very Sicki.
I'd like to give you a shot of two kid, but I'm not a sadist.
although some lousy poets have painted me as such
with the brush of jealousy and ignorance. Bastards!

So, listen-up kid. You really don't want to write like me.
You've got your own podium and pedestal to tame,
here in the dream and also there outside the dream.
You just have to know it. I mean really know it and own it.
Show you've got the jam, and what it takes kid.
Show you've got the goods. And then it's no holds barred.

So, Tally-Ho kid! Mount up! Hot spur your pony and pen
and ride hell bent for leather. Cross the finish line first.
I've always maintained second is sooooo over rated.

I thanked him very much and shook his hand
Suddenly a magical pony appeared at my side
I mounted up and raced past the wind,
and over the finish line first,
faster than you could say Al Purdy!.

I looked back at Al who was wildly clapping
and shouting at the top of his lungs ...
"It's not a one-trick pony.
Keep ridin' kid! Keep ridin'!"

From Poetry to Zen and Back

It's been said that the art of poetry is, at its best,
when it says what otherwise can't be said.
Did I really just say that?
I would apologize for the very abstract talk,
but the problem is I'm not sorry.
Did I really just say that? Guess so. Not sorry!

The appeal of poetic words isn't all that different
from the appeal of Zen. How so you ask?
It may take 3 seconds or it may take 30 years
but the key for both these BIGGIES
is to not to wind the watch with too much might.
After all, we would never want to be accused of gilding the lily
or worse yet, electronic sadism. Would we? Don't ask.
Please don't ask. I cannot tell a lie.
Did I really just say that? Zen eet must be true. Mebbee.

My next question is about the guy who decided \it would
be a good idea to put legs on a serpent.
Isn't that just a lizard at that point?
You'll notice I didn't call that creepy thing a snake.
Why? You might wish you hadn't asked that question.

The reason I don't like the 'sn" word related to a creepy crawly
is because "sn" makes me think of sneezing and right now
I'm thinking of sneezing little baby sn*k*s
from the double breathing portals centered on my face.
Actually makes me want to puke razor blades!
I want to scream out a GO to that intelligent guy.
Hurry up! Put them legs on those goddamned reptiles,
I'm sure that would put my worst nightmares to rest.
I can't visualize a lizard fitting up my breathing portals.
But enough about distasteful things. I've better things to discuss.

Back to Poetry and Zen. They are really brothers in dreams,
sisters in sentience and comrades in spirit
creating, shaping and conquering minds and worlds:

Inner worlds, where all outer worlds and physical manifestations
are first imagined and visualized and created in 3-D thought patterns
before they are out-pictured into the concrete world.

Poetry is the beautification of human thought and emotion.
It takes the reader on journey beyond worlds
It soothes the shattered soul and mends the troubled mind.
It heals the tattered ruins of a broken heart.
It is the true salve to assuage the wounded spirit.
Poetry: a world without it is beyond imagination.
Zen is the calm inside the peaceful. The empathy within the love.
The cleansing of the soul. The rising of the spirit
It takes the reader on a journey through the cosmos:
Dharma, Nirvana Eternity, then back to Soul.
It brings eternity into the here and now so we can touch it.
It turns the heart into a lotus flower, opening to everyone.
It is the true path to knowledge and enlightenment.
Zen: meditation and intuition to elevate the cosmos.

Exiting the cloud cover of the deep, I take a deep breath.
I sit back in my pilot's seat and pick up the microphone.

This is your captain speaking.
We are almost at our destination.

Please disembark in an orderly fashion, as I know you will,
with true understanding, calm and empathy
for your fellow passengers disembarking with you.

I hope you enjoyed the trip
from Poetry to Zen and back.

Who is Grady Lewis Anyway?

Another cluster of random letters
in a certain fast forward reversible order
with a veracity of vowels and critical consonants
that will make sense to fellow humans
that travel the same wavelengths and sonic curvatures
as Sensei and the Professor.

It's the best they can do at this juncture of mind
until they can communicate with a higher intelligence.
But they probably have lifetimes of work to do before
they're even considered novices in that higher realm.

Until then...
Sensei and the Professor
have only these words to offer you.
This and a bowl full of gratitude
for listening to our poems
while we are honing our skills
readying ourselves for that big audition in the sky,
That big word festival of dreams and poetry
hosted by none other than Grady Lewis.

If you're wondering who Grady Lewis is,
then you haven't read enough poetry
from the realms one step beyond.

When you take that step
Grady, Sensei and the Professor
will be there to welcome you
with open recitations.

Disney Out-Takes

I wonder what Mickey & Minnie Mouse are up to tonight.
Are they dodging cats, playing tag?
Or could they be munching on cheese morsels?
Maybe they're talking on the telephone to Pluto.
Maybe they're snuggled up together watching their favourite hero,
Mighty Mouse on their big screen TV, as he saves the day once again.
Maybe they're playing sabotage the mouse trap
or hide and seek with Tweety and Sylvester.
They might even just be sitting silently,
twiddling their paws or twitching their whiskers.
Maybe they are sitting in a remote tropical vista,
somewhere on vacation and being bloody boring.
So the Mickster and Minns will have to take a back seat for now.
Fade into the pixels of the page, so to speak... or not speak.

SLO-MO FADE OUT AND CUT TO THE DUCKS

Unca Scrooge is in his counting house stacking up his gold.
Donald in his gambling hat is betting at the track.
Huey, Duey and Luey are terrorizing the local pond as usual.
And everything seems just ducky. Hunky dory ducky actually.
...BORING. But hark. a familiar sound ...

SCREEN FADE OUT TO AUDIO OVERLAY AND FADE IN

 "Ahh What's up Doc?" chomp, chomp, chomp.
By ! It's Bugs, and Elmer is closing in quickly
on the fruitless, continuous-loop hunt again!
Elmer's going more insane with every failed rabbit hunt
and is constantly repeating "Where is that goofy wabbit?"
And now to really corkscrew things up royally
Goofy and Daffy just crashed the wrong set for the 2nd time.
Now they're yapping in riddles with no answers... typical.
Goofy is like Jughead of the Archie and Veronica scene.
And Daffy is like the smart assed Reggie of the comic strip.
If things get any more ridiculously out of hand, we'll need help.
Where in hell is Yosemite Sam anyway.

He's the always absentee, overpaid security on this back lot.
It's all too much rigamarole, hassle. Too much goofiness
A lovely walk in the park gone very, very wrong.

After all these shenanigans and out takes,
I'm still wondering what Mickey and Minnie are up to.
What are they doing right now?

Whatever it is, it must be more interesting
than what I'm doing right now, which is ...
wondering what they're doing.

FADE TO BLACK.

To Sup of the Universal Language

We catch up with The Professor at the corner of Itch and Scratch.
Right across the street from the "Hungry Eye" flashing neon sign.

The Professor is currently gnawing and nibbling the corners
of an 8-year-old, finely aged, Vermont, extra sharp cheddar block.
He picked it up on his way to work but couldn't wait to get there
so he cracked the bright orange block open in his car
and started gnawing ferociously on it at a red light.

The lady in the car next to him was gawking at him googly-eyed,
staring at him like she couldn't believe what she was seeing.
She had a "what's wrong with that guy" kind of face evolving.
The Professor, being a gourmand and good Samaritan and all,
held the block of cheese out the window in a gesture of good will
offering her a bite of the vintage, gourmet block of cheese.
She must have taken the gesture as an act of aggression
because she peeled out and ran the red light to get away from him.

"How could anyone see something as fine as 8-year aged cheddar
as a sign of aggression" he wondered, totally astonished.
Pondering this made his whiskers twitch and itch so he scratched,
which seemed very fitting at the corner of Itch and Scratch.
The light turned green. The Professor turned left and that felt right,
so he continued on his cheesy way. As was usually the way with him.
He slowly disappeared into the fog of the day he was pursuing
which would lead him invariably into the tender night. He hoped.

As for Sensei, she was keeping busy as a bee with six stingers
doing nothing much in the eyes of the average beholder
but in actuality she was building a particle soul-accelerator
that would remain attached to the body, but travel elsewhere too.
Both body and spirit, self and soul, communicating flawlessly
through a series of hyper-sensitive extra sensory synapses,
would be totally aware of each other in two places at the same time.
She had successfully built a new lever of unconscious consciousness.
She had The Professor to thank for opening her mind to new thought.
She was pleased with this creation of a double life scenario

viewable by both body and soul concurrently and interchangeably.
It would be the true essence of sane Schizophrenia at its best!

After sweating it out for the Universal Gipper this morning,
she decided to take a well-deserved break and do a test run.
She attached the imaginary mind wires to her real forehead
and threw the on-switch and off she went ...part of her anyway.
Her soul was flying through star clusters and space dust
at hypersonic light year speeds. She was so enjoying the speed.
She didn't want to land anywhere. The speed was exhilarating!
She was so wrapped up in it she didn't notice the scenery at all.
Worlds being born. Worlds dying. She missed it all.

Being both virtually and intrinsically attached to her body,
she was able to hear the phone ringing back home.
She could even see the number that was calling her.
Damn! Wouldn't you know it, mother again,
calling at yet another most inconvenient time.
Oh well, being the dutiful and respectful daughter
she had recently forced herself to become,
she pulsed back home in a nano-second
and picked up the noisily intrusive landline telephone.
"What is it Mom?" she queried in a forced but gentle voice
trying to hide her extreme annoyance at this interruption
to her enjoyable speed sprint though the multiverses.

Silence for a second and then maniacal laughter.
"Bahahaha. Fooled ya Sensei" bellowed the erudite Professor.
"Come back immediately Sensei. Even faster than that.
What a fabulous happening I have to share!
I've just made contact with the parallel Sensei and Professor
from the 7th Dimension of the 3rd cluster of the 11th universe.

Sensei was elated, electrified and absolutely ecstatic.
"I'll be right there ... before you can say Schizo.
Actually I'm right here now. Turn around Prof.
He turned around and his face cracked like an egg and broke into
the most colourful high pixel smile he'd ever smiled.
They spent the next momentary eternity speaking of:
Dimensions and dreams, screamers and caterwaulers.

Cowboys and Indians, horses of odd colours and dog-eyed cats.
Schizoids and manics, elations and depressions.
Ghosts and poltergeists, interlopers and doppelgangers
and Senseis and Professors of the 4th kind.

What a day it was. What a life it was.
Sensei and The Professor poured themselves
a big bolt of nano-wine concentrate
and with a gleam to the future in their eyes
they lifted their goblets, flipped the travel switch on,
blasted off in a blaze of synaptic glory
and flew into momentary eternity once again,
to sup of the universal knowledge.

Innocent Bystanders

The big iron stamp clanged down
onto the paper covered steel desk.
And then the strict forceful voice
leaking onto the black and white TV screen
"What you are about to see is a true story.
Only the names have been changed to protect the innocent."
Makes me wonder why they never changed the names
of the bystanders. I gotta ask sans expecting an answer.

Da da ta da… fade in to Sgt Joe Friday
Slicked back greasy kid stuff hair and beady eyes;
a strange lookin' dude at best. Dumbo at worst.
Def not a pin-up boy heart-throb.
A bit lazy too. Friday only worked on Fridays,
At least in my area on my small, black &white screen, world.
I heard via the grapevine he was a real Prima Donna.
Thought his breath was rosy and his armpits didn't stink
and figured the only day worthy of his presence
was his namesake day of the week … Friday.
He caught a lot of bad guys, but I don't think he killed any.

The good guys and the bad guys took it up a step, back then.
Actually cared about innocent bystanders, back then.
Times and criminals were much more civilized in his day.
He was a no nonsense, standup guy. Had a good record.

Speaking of records… who coulda, woulda' thought
little Willie Shatner would cut a disc after he left Star Trek?
He should have slipped a disc instead of cutting one.
That operation would have been much more successful.
I mean, crikey mate, I couldn't believe how bad it was
and how ridiculously crazy he looked promoting it on TV.
And then, like a disease, Leonard Nimoy follows suit.
Didn't they give a damn about us innocent bystanders?
Were they that nuts or just plain money hungry?

Speaking of Leonard Nimoy, I went to a random art exhibit

in Northampton, Massachusetts a few years back and would you
believe it was all photographs taken by Spock himself.
I had no idea a Vulcan could even use a camera.
And that wasn't even the crazy part.
What struck me as wonderfully odd was,
all his photos were of nude woman. I kid you not.
The gallery was like a high brow nudie bar.
And in my very amateur, innocent bystander opinion
the pictures were fantastic.

We're all voyeurs, even when we're not.
We're all wanna-be's, even when we're not.
We're all good guys, even when we're not.

Bystanders of all ilk and fashion:
Trystanders, Shystanders and Crystanders
And the biggie of biggies...Innocent bystanders.

Ah yes, truth be told ...
we're all innocent bystanders ...
until we're not.

Do You Know the Type?

Some people carry things real heavy like.
And for days on end too.
It seems almost the preferred method for them.
Perhaps they haven't mastered the art of not pressing it.
Or maybe haven't even heard of the concept.
I feel for them; you know?
Their nerves all racked and packed into their souls
like in a King Oscar can of sardines.
I want so badly to just lift the little pull tab
to the space that houses their essence
and I want to tip in a fifth of bourbon.

I want to hum Miles' entire 'Kind of Blue' album
directly into their aching neurotransmitters.

Don't get me wrong, I'm one of them too.
Nervous by nature. Mispronounced by name.
Maybe that's why I feel for them so. I feel for me too.
Do you know the type I'm talking about?

Let me tell you what it seems to me we're like.
We're like a strangulated version of a deep inhalation
that seems to suck itself out as it's heading in.
We're like a bunch of persistent hiccups
with no water fountain is sight. My kingdom for a spot of wat!
We're like a winning lottery ticket with an ink spill
blotting out one or more numbers
to make it just another weepsy-wopsy loser.
We're like a driverless car with three armless drivers
and two steering wheels that turn left and one turning right.
And actually, it doesn't turn left it turns wrong says the right.
Yeah, that's right says the left... and there you have it.
Just another pile of crap and what if isms
to be analyzed in a mind squandering dance of the veils.
The ones we never saw that were referred to, subliminally,
in the show 'The Day of the Triffids'. (a 'B' movie)
But here back in our 'C' movie lives,

heavy doom and gloom hang over some people
and they can never seem to wring the clouds out.
The wet and the tears just keep building up inside.
So they try to construct imaginary fail-safe dams
to hold in all the sorrow and rage in
as they try to master the art of not pressing it.

They're finally getting it. Understanding the concept a bit.
But try as they may, they just can't master it ... I feel for them.
Their nerves jumping and twitching and kicking.
They need to unrack and unpack their stilted souls.
Time to leave the tin can of repressed desires.
Time to pull that rusted imprisoning tab right off.
No worries about the cuts ... and band-aids be damned!
Just pour some alcohol on it. The cure for all wounds.

These type of people need to walk a mile or seventy with me
so I can show them how to smile and wink convincingly
and directly into their semi-comatose neurotransmitters.

Nervous by nature. Name often mispronounced.
Maybe that's why I feel for us.
Do you know the type I'm talking about?

Bet'cha do!

Look and See

Look, I told her.
I'm figuring it out as I go too. Same as you.
I've heard plenty of probablys and finallys myself.
Regardless, the sea will always eclipse the wave every time.
It would be such a folly to fight nature.

Look, I told her.
You may have heard this even before you heard this but,
there's plenty of everything for everyone if people would share.
As we sit here scraping for these few things
there are people somewhere drinking 600-dollar bottles of wine
and leaving most of it on the table.
Can you believe that?

Look, she told me.
If it's too much to behold, feel free to look away.
I want to do this thing as naturally as I can.
I mean, they sculpted The Splendid Baldachin
in 1690 and it still stands today.
So there has to be an open language to the whole thing
if you really want it to last.

Look, I told her.
I'm figuring it out as I go too. Same as you.
Regardless, the heart will always eclipse the head every time.
It would be such a folly to fight love.

Look and See, she told me,
widening her left eye and squinting her right,
if you're not in it for love ...
then I'm outta here
and you'll be long gone ...
yeah, just another long gone lonesome daddy.

And hey ... don't let the door hit you
on your way out of the us we almost were.

Realization Departed

There's a contrast between the two.
The wrong question and the right answer.
Is that too basic a comparison?

Ok, how's this?
Is it true that no matter how much rain falls
there's bound to be a sunny day eventually?
Is that better? No?

Fine, here's another attempt.
Is it in fact shame on me
if I find myself bamboozled by the same thing
a second time ad infinitum? Yes, that's it.
So ... now that we have that squared away
let me move on to the next uncertainty.

When absolutely nothing works, where are you then?
And can 'nothing' ever work. I don't think so.
But something can always work. No food stamps for something
But lots of stimulus cheques and food stamps for nothing.
And what good is a barrier with no gate
if you hope to one day roam free? Now you see, right?

It's quite an extraordinary phenomenon. Reminds me of when I read
the entire collected discourses of Sir Humphry Davy.
What a laugh... what a gas. It was nitrous delight in drag.
All he wanted was to be buried where he died.
That can't be too much to ask, right?
Well ... maybe too much to ask if he died
in a hospital elevator or in a posh uptown bar toilet.

There's a similarity between the two.
The wrong answer and the right question.
But mostly it's buried too deep in opposing layers
for us to actually see it. Realization departed long, long ago.
You do see that, right? Right?

Key to the Secret

It's so odd that when you put letters in a certain pattern
it makes sense to me.
And it makes sense to you...sometimes.
Words, man.
Words.
I love them.

The same way philosophers love suppositions.
The same way astronomers love star clustered spaces.
The same way drama queens love entanglements.
Seriously, man. I love words.
That much.

It's so odd that a person can maintain
an all or nothing state for that many years.
But that makes sense to me...maybe to you too.
Extremes, man.
Extremes.
I'm predisposed to them.

The same way a devotee is predisposed to monastic states.
The same way a pilgrim on an LSD journey is predisposed
to lucid dreams and experiences.
The same way a practitioner of mysticism is predisposed
to being very open to the majestic of the mystic.
Seriously, man. Just like that.

It's odd the way things can transport you to yesterday.
Just like that. times, ages, feelings
Memories man ...
Suddenly you're gone. You're there again, but you're not.
Time travelling standing still not moving, but moving.
The same way a song can transport you back to love.
The same way a movie can transport you back to heartache.
The same way a funeral can transport you to a different death.
The same way a birth can transport you to your baby days.

Words.
I love to play with them, scramble them, coddle them.
And cajole them into helping me build a masterpiece.
I love them and they know it.

Extremes
I love to go to extremes, live on the edge, tempt fate.
And generally throw caution to the wind
I love extremes and they know it.

Memories
I love to sway on their wings of laughter and tears.
And everything else in between.
I love memories and they know it.

Words. Extremes. Memories.
Mix them all together
and love them... I mean really love them.
And they will love you back
and give you the key to the secret.

And the secret will set you free.

In Between the Yawning and the Yawning

What people fail to realize is that my sensei
is quite the gumshoe to boot.
And she has this house full of vintage detective novels,
comic books, astronomy, and mysticism.
I mean floor to ceiling in each room, just covered.
And I'll tell you another thing, see.
She's never one to lack heart, see.
And you best not forget she's equally seasoned
in her skills with the blade and with the barrel etc.

I'll never forget this mystery she solved for me once.
Every time I would ride a roller coaster
I would begin to uncontrollably yawn.
One after another. For the entire ride.
Then sure enough, when the coaster cart
made its way back to home base,
the yawning would stop.

When I told her this, she told me her story (true)
On a bright moonlit day in the mountains
She was sunning herself relaxingly comfortable
beside the purple lake of flowering heads.
All alone. Nobody else around. Absolute silence abounding.
She was almost asleep when she heard a super loud yawning.
Where was it coming from? She was alone or so she thought.
Eyes peeled and darting she saw the waters of the lake
rise up in the centre and form a purple mouth.
Then the mouth opened wide and yawned loudly.
This event repeated thrice in succession and then abated.
It never happened again that day, but on every future visit
the purple lake of flowering heads would repeat the same sequence.

One time she had a harrowing experience at the lake.
The water of the lake formed a living swirling sword in the stone
and the lake whispered loudly then softly, over and over again …
'Remember King Arthur'… 'Remember King Arthur.'
She bowed down in reverence and asked the lake

why she needed to remember King Arthur.
The lake then produced the form of a bootleg whiskey barrel
with a scimitar resting on top of the unopened barrel
and the lake whispered in guttural thrusts,
'Remember prohibition'... 'Remember prohibition.'

Then she told me, in order to flow with the yawning
and gain forbidden knowledge and true enlightenment,
I must read 'The Holographic Universe'.
And then in order to understand the yawning,
I must read 'Einstein's Monster' and 'Gravity's Engines'.

She said she was searching for a book the lake had whispered of.
'The Width of Fermot's Black Hole Tamed by a Courageous Star',
It was written in the 7th Dimension of White Holes
and is currently and partisanly banned in that realm.
The lake didn't give her directions as to where to find the book
but she is hopeful it will as time elapses
and it fully gains total confidence in her loyalty
and recognizes the purity and unselfishness of her motives.

Sensei said the main things to remember
and take lessons from were:

King Arthur. Prohibition.
The sword in the stone.
The blade and the barrel.
The black hole and the star.

She went on to stress the need to quest onward with gusto,
to gain the confidence of a secluded lake of my choice
and to always listen to the lake when it whispered.
Sensei said the best enlightenment is available and free
if we listen openly, ardently and alertly
to the lake as it whispers and yawns,
releasing the messages, parables and truisms
enfolded and unfolded
in between the yawning... and the yawning.

The Finest of Lines

It's the finest of lines:
That distinction between
mental illness and brilliance.
So many of the greats throughout history have been labeled
"crazy" or "quirky" or "cuckoo for cocoa puffs".
Genius is rarely understood or accepted in its own time.
It takes decades. Sometimes centuries.
For the masses to appreciate genius.
In many cases they're forgotten over time by most.
And that's ok. Because the shine they shone
when they were here and shining, is the point of the whole thing.

It's like the song that tries to persuade genius to come out:
"This little light of mine. I'm gonna let it shine."
There are so many potential bright and brilliant lights
Oh me oh my I say. Why, why, why don't they shine???

Here's a scenario:
We've probably all been guilty of this at some time.
I mean, we can be living right next door to a genius
and swear to God he's a goofball or a dolt.
We can't see the writing on the wall for the wallpaper
and we can't see the genius of others through our cataracts.
And yes, we do have invisible cataracts
that only let us see what we want to see,
and heaven forbid we see genius in someone else,
as that would just diminish our ego. Our sense of self.
That's the kind of cuckoo caca we seem to be mired in.
Quicksand of the mind. Handcuffed integrity.
Stuck in the clutch of false witness and pre-judgement.

It's the finest of lines:
The difference between
courage, bravery and true grit.
It's fantastically fascinating to look back in time
and see who history has labeled a hero of a villain.
Or a hero as a villain and a villain as a hero.

It does happen you know. We are easily duped.
That still holds very true today. Like amen in the church.
But I can see through the many, many guises.
Oh yeah, believe you me, I can see right down
to the narrow of the bone, the marrow of it all.
My ability to do so did take time to cultivate.
Maybe it's been decades. Maybe centuries.
Maybe lifetimes on end never-ending.
I can't even be sure how long I've been lolling around
in this laughing gas bubble of the multi-verse.

Here's another scenario:
Let's say God loved bubble wands and blowing bubbles,
and he loved spinning in circles wand waving
as all the bubbles dispersed across the great nothingness.
And as they dispersed their outer shells hardened
and their insides became very dense over time.
And after floating for centuries, a group of them
began revolving around the biggest one of their group.
They became planets spinning around the 'Big Boy'.
The star we, in our little corner of the 'verse' call the sun.
Or Sol, or that big fireball of nuclear energy in the sky
that keeps us from freezing our asses off and dying,
and yet one day it will fry us all as it goes supernova.
So much for God's children. They've been bad.
Now classed as irredeemable ... Incinerate them!.
And then imagine God getting bored of the game,
and throwing his wand into the universal garbage can
when his bottle of soapy liquid ran empty.
And then when he heard his mother calling him for dinner,
he left the general area and we, his creations,
future living breathing bubble babies,
just kept on spinning away and further away
until we were lost little lambs
who couldn't find their way home.
You can believe that's true or you can deny it.
Who's to say it's wrong? Who's to say it's right?

It's the finest of lines:
The difference between believer and agnostic.

The believer:
Believing in an afterlife.
A beautiful eternal life.

The agnostic:
Believing in a nothing after. Just total black unconsciousness.

One is right and one is wrong.

The believer doesn't care,
because if it's not true,
he'll never know the difference.

The agnostic, being a non-believer,
will be totally screwed.
If he's wrong, he'll be banned
and won't be allowed to enter
through the hallowed doors to eternity,
because he doesn't have a ticket to ride
and the glory train won't pass his way again.

Yes. It's the finest of lines:
A happy, raving, saved fanatic.
Or a lost, left out in the cold, poor bastard.

Deviate the Levitate

Why so scared to deviate, huh?
Worried it might all come undone in a day?
Crumble, fall down like London Bridge?
Didn't Bobby McFerrin say "Don't worry...be happy"?
Didn't Bukowski craft his first poem on a computer?
At 70 years of age? What a brave guy. Still had all his marbles.
Kept playing the game and kept winning, winning, winning,
as the whacky-assed Charlie Sheen would yappity-yap off.
Wasn't Double Trouble born of wit and whimsy?
'Though some folks say it was born of insanity and genius.
And just so you know, the history books have painted
an extensively incomplete and one-sided picture of most things.
The truth is actually more likely to be found
in the places no one wants to look.

Take this for example.
The importance of staying humble within the struggle
is rarely noted, spoken of or even whispered about.
The fact that it was all based on luck and chance
basically goes unacknowledged most of the time.

Why so scared to levitate, huh?
It's not like there's a mathematical exactitude to the thing.
We all go as high as we were meant to fly.
Or as high as the ladder of belief allows us to climb.
It's that simple and it's also more complex than that.
The energies are flowing all the time.
North and south. East and west. Yin and yang
Bitter and sweet all of them becoming more than they are:
Northeast; Southwest yinyang, .and bittersweet.

Characteristically and through the ages,
it's all harmonious, integrated and integral.
And when the Rastafari people ask
if you understand a concept they ask, "seen"?
So just answer "Yeah, seen".
I don't know about you, but myself

and thousands of Parkinson's disease sufferers
see ghosts all the time ... well, a lot of the time.
They see them and I see them
and I don't even have Parkinson's disease.
But I can truthfully and emphatically scream
at the top of my being "SEEN".

Mebbee we are only supposed to see spirit things
and ghosts and not material object things.
Seeing a real object thing could be construed as "ob-seen"
Never mind. Not so. File it under irrelevant.
I'm just in the middle of a big digression
where thoughts rush in so fast they get tangled up
in a potpourri of inane and nonsensical broken mind cookies.

I want to deviate. I want to levitate
I want to rise up with my floating ghosts
and visit the lands of lore they tell me about.
I want to levitate all things to me.
Instead of having them levitate me to them.

I know I shouldn't do it, but I'm going to do it anyway.
The next smiling ghost I see floating overhead,
I'm going to deviate and grab onto his coat-tails
and go with him to the land of knowing
so I can learn by osmosis to levitate without fear.
I want to be able to deviate the levitate.

I don't want to be scared anymore:
To fly on my own volition.
To yell out "SEEN"
To deviate the levitate.

Don't. Just Don't

Don't blame the past.
And don't blame the present for the past.
It's just like sending telegrams and toothpicks,
from the same time and the same forest,
to different clocks and different tree farms.
Like zoning out the zones you're stuck in
that don't fit and dismantling and reshaping them
into wristwatches and necklace timepieces.
Faux, knockoff Apple, Mac, Cartier and Rolex.
Then selling them as the real thing for the big bucks.
C'mon man. Give me a break... and don't call me Joe.
Don't! Just don't.

Don't blame your hands or eyes.
And don't blame the paint, the brush or the canvas.
They can't make a masterpiece by themselves.
It's got to be a joint effort of all five plus your creativity.
And don't say you have none. Everyone has creativity.
It is part of the human genome, spirit and psyche.
It's been that way for forever.
You know what they say...the greater the artistry,
the greater the underlying phenomenon.
So grab your long buried phenomena
and hidden creativity by the scruff of their necks
and plop them down with paint, brush and canvas
at the altar of greatness and art.
The Bride, creativity, will arrive at the altar
to stand in obedience to your desire
and when the marriage is consummated
with the blend of paint, brush, canvas and creativity
kiss the muse of inspiration in reverence
and your masterpiece will come, kicking and screaming,
into your newly designed world.
And the you, you were always meant to be,
will be born and then ... born again and again
into the colours of your soul.
Don't count on being spellbound and remaining so.

Get rid of the lollipops and clouds in your head.
Pretending space isn't there doesn't make it not be there.
Just like pretending to be a 7 footer
won't make you any taller.
Maybe your head will hold itself a bit higher.
And maybe your shoulders
will carry themselves a bit broader.
But that's about it.

Now, I'm not saying that's nothing.
It's something. And so is the new you.
Don't ever doubt it.
Don't. Just don't.

Oh yeah.
And give me a break man,
don't ever call me Joe!

Don't! Just don't.

Extraordinary? Perhaps. Probably

Is the vanilla that comes from Madagascar
really the best? Perhaps.
Is the cold-pressed extra-virgin olive oil from Tunisia
really the best? Probably.
Is it really best to be strange and original?
It would seem so.
Is it still paranoia if it's true?
Probably not.
Is it a sign of things to come
when my cat sits on my stacks of paper as I write?
Perhaps she understands.
God, I hope so!

Reality may have slipped off again, but wouldn't you say
Nostradamus was actually quite accurate in his prophecies?
I'm not claiming to be well-versed
in all the ins and outs of his predictions.
But I am saying he must have gotten it right,
once in a while, to still be spoken of today
and to end up in this poem.
That's kind of extraordinary.
Right?

Extraordinary?. Perhaps. Probably.

Pardon Me. Excuse Me. Allow Me.

Pardon me.
I'm just passing through.
On my way I hope not to miss too many meals.
But can you believe people starve to death every day
on this rock we call home?
When's the last time we spoke of such things though?
Look, I don't want to be a downer.
In fact...I've been called the life of the party
more often than not. I just feel that's worth noting.

Excuse me.
I'm just observing a thing here and a thing there.
So, were any of us around at the time?
When it all started?
I saw this documentary once
that broke the whole thing down into 2 hours.
No lie!

All 13.7 billion years ... squeezed it right in there.
Inside that paltry unsuspecting 2 hours.
What a trip that was!
That was the first time I remember hearing the word "hellish."
I wondered why they used that word.
It all looked so beautiful.

Allow me.
Would you believe that I gave away
937 pieces of my artwork in the last few months?
Like, I really gave it all away.
I'd wanted to for so long
but something kept me tethered. Attached.
And then one day it just opened up, wide,
and became a new thing.
The craziest thing is,
I never felt like they were really even mine ...
until the moment I gave them away.
I'm just passing through my passing thoughts:

You never miss the water 'til the well runs dry.
You never miss a meal 'til you're starving to death.
You never miss the years 'til the days burn away.
You never miss the minutes 'til the hours run out.
You never miss your paintings 'til the walls are bare.

Oh yeah, pardon me, excuse me.
Allow me to mention one more thing worth noting.

You're always the life of the party ...
until you're not.

Human Supposition

I'd like to join them.
If they are heading the way me and sensei are heading.
I'd like to feel any sensation whatsoever.
So long as it feels good. Is that hedonistic of me?
No more so than an impatient driver
trying to distance herself from traffic.

Look, I accept that things can't always feel good.
But when they do, we need to hang onto them.
And I do know all the little sounds of spring
are always well received. by me and sensei.
Especially the sound of a hard April rain on a tin roof
or a soft summer breeze on thin sheer curtains.

I'd like to become the essence of all elements
and intellectually spar gently with them
as rain with the sea and air with the clouds.
I'd love to mind-meld with the distant erudite Roshi.
I'd love to know who they think we were
before we were conceived in this incarnation.

I'd like to know the answers to the unknowable:
As time goes by does it go by the same for everyone,
Is every day somehow the same on the quantum level?
Is, everywhere static in one location called everywhere?
Is it on our rock the same as it is on others
in the Milky Way? In the Universe? In the Multiverse?
Are the questers, on distant planets, asking the same questions
we are asking here in our little corner of the Unbounded?

These are the thoughts that come to mind.
whenever I think about how I'm able to think.
I've been trying to walk out of myself into my other self
but I can't resolve the fractal difference between me and me.
What kind of situation is this? It's human supposition ...
I suppose.
But Not for Me

The jailhouse could never be for me.
Unless the bars call out just enough for me to hear them.
Oh wait...I was confused.
Wrong kind of bars.

Ok, let's try this again.
The dry tank could never be for me.
Unless the powers that be decide it is.
But if that's the case, you better believe
I'm going on the run the wet for a little while yet.
Some days are diamonds. Some days are dust.
Some nights are moonstone. Some nights are rust.
Sometimes I can't tell the difference.
Usually after running too much of the wet.
Does that make more sense?
No? Ok, no problem.
Try this one on for size.

The struggle with one's own self
can never be won so why fight?
Everyone seems so knowledgeable. So there.
They all always seem to know their threshold.
I just haven't arrived there yet.
Probably never will.

Jailhouses, dry tanks and known thresholds
may be fine for some...
But not for me.

Old Irish Me and My Kazoo

I was eating a Philly cheesesteak the other day.
But I wasn't in Philadelphia. I was in a laundromat
reflecting on the vast amount of hours and days
I've spent in laundromats in my life.
Then I remembered I couldn't count that high in my head.
So I dropped that thought.

I've never been to Philadelphia but it's on my bucket list.
But not because of their world-famous cheesesteaks.
It's on my list because they have an unexpectedly big plethora
of oddity shops in the city, and I'll fit right in. A human oddity.
And, I'm a lifelong fan of the oddities of life.
If I ever make it to the City of Brotherly Love
I'll try to hook-up with a Twisted Sister for a bite to eat.
Probably swing by Geno's and grab a cheesesteak.
I would certainly have mine with Cheese Whiz.
One of the good things about being from the poor side.
you try things the rich folks never seem to buy
and it turns out they're the ones missing out on a good thing.
I mean, seriously, who in their right mind
picks provolone over Cheese Whiz?
Right now I'm wondering why they call it "whiz" but I digress.
So, back to laundromats. My coin and metal-darling stewards.

If you are going to be in the business of washing clothes
I would hope you have a sense of humor about you.
And if you, like me, have been forced to be a laundromat regular
throughout your life then you damn sure better have
a good sense of humor about life, soap, clothes and people.
I've washed my knickers and unmentionables
at places like The Lost Sock, Permanently Pressed,
Spot On Spot Off, Cheapo Cleaners, Missing Buttons
and The Dirty Dog...just to name a few.
The best are always the 24 hour Mat shops.
There is nothing better than people-watching
at a laundromat at midnight. Or two in the morning.
These folks are a special breed of hobo cat,

the kind who bring out all their dirty little bits
hoping nobody will be watching them load into the washer.

One time I was there at 3 A.M, just mindin' my own
when a hefty, built like a brick shithouse, gal came in
with a couple of bags of laundry. I was watching her.
Not for any other reason than just honest to god boredom.
She turned to me and said, in a harsh Irish brogue,
"What you starin' at commie?" I was delighted.
I jumped up, and in one swift motion pulled out my kazoo.
"Take a listen to this Old Irish!" I shuffled a few moonwalk steps
and then I started belting out a jammed up version
of the old jam tart song "Irish Washer Woman"
She immediately started to River Dance to the beat.
By the time our laundromat duties were completed
we were the best of cymbalic and imbecilic friends.
Or so I thought, but alas, alak … I never saw her again.

Being the sentimental, slightly mental fool I am,
I still go to the laundromat at 3 AM to do my laundry
hoping someday she'll appear out of the blue
and I can pull out my old kazoo again
and rock her socks off to the beat of my drum …
the one I now carry in my huge stretched-out back pocket.
I never should have kept it there as it's thrown my back out
and bent my hip so my left leg is shorter than the right.
This makes me look a bit gimpy when I walk
and my walk always imprints a wedgie in my ass.
But it's too late to change pockets now.
If I did, I'd shorten the other leg and then I'd lose a full inch…
an inch I can't afford to lose.
But I've got moxie….true grit. I'm in it for the long haul.
I've been spending so much time and money at the Mat
I could have bought a share in it by now. But, I didn't.
I was, and still am, too busy practicing my kazoo and waiting …
waiting for Old Irish to show up again.

The Universe Will

I've spent my life being the exception to rules.
The difficulty of it was always outweighed by
the pleasure in allowing life to run on all by itself.
Who am I to interfere with the will of the universe?
What of free will you ask?
Well...I did get that tattooed on my hands.
So there's that.

I'm just saying it's been my experience
when I live from a place of trust and oneness my life works.
When I live from a place of doubt and separation...not so much.

Ok, what was the question again?
Oh yeah, how did it start between the two of us?
Well ... I called and she answered.
That's the short cut, bottom line version.
Here's how it really happened...

Three or four lifetimes ago.
Or maybe three or four dimensions away from here.
Either way, it was another space and another time.

I was minding my own business
just be-boppin' down the street
when she roller skated through my legs
to the song Ramalama Ding Dong
in an amazing acrobatic feat of speed and accuracy.

Somehow, she managed to move most of her bod
into another dimension to allow her
to be only 1 inch wide
so she could shock the shit out of me
with her acrobatics.
And she did.
I nearly had a heart attack. But I didn't.
Not in the medical sense, but I did in the emotional sense.
She had me at the first waft of breeze from her skates.

Man ... that really did if for me.
I mean, really
how forward can a person get.
Almost touching, but not.

So, long story short, we married yet again
for the umpteenth dozen time.
Some say a fool never learns.
I say a wise many always remembers.

And boy, oh boy, did I remember.
And life just keeps on rolling by all by itself
to the will of the universe.

If you can't remember who you are
what you should be doing
or who you always belong to,
the universe will.

No worries Buds ...
the universe will.

What Happens is This

What happens is this.
You're asked to be perfectly sincere.
Then you're judged for it.
What sense does that make?

What happen is this.
You're asked to be absolutely genuine.
Then you're ridiculed for it.
Apparently, people don't appreciate honesty.

I once fell into an emersion therapy of my own devising.
Not even on purpose. Happenstance, you know?
An instinctual inclination said it would work
but I would have to do it 3 times.
Sure, I thought. That's doable.

So, I played 'Rock, Paper Scissors'
with my critical doppelganger frenemy
to find the preferred order of attack.
The best way to start the emersion.

Rock.
So I thought about a black onyx alien stone
flecked with glittering bits of Lapis and diamonds.
I concentrated and entered the rock becoming one with it.
The obsidian gleam of pulsating brain was mesmerizing.
The Lapis and diamonds blinked off and on like eyes.
Actually they were eyes, but they were blind.
They were only speckled on the onyx for show.
I felt the warmth of the dark and the cool ice
of the gemstones cutting into my mind
and filling it with ancient lore and images.
It was so beautiful I thought I had died
until I came-to while exiting the Rock
and moving onto the second emersion.

Paper.

Okay, now I was in my element. This should be easy.
It was and it wasn't. I entered the paper easily,
but it was so hard to navigate the pixels and the grain.
Up, down, sideways. Over, under, above and below.
Pixels were spinning, spinning, spinning
and turning me into words, sentences, and poetry.
The ink from my mind ran onto the paper
in a technicolour waterfall of bliss
but as it hit the paper the colors coalesced and became black.
I realized intrinsically and emphatically
the black and white of the world was multicoloured
and the colours were just the ultimate of black and white
Ebony and pearl were opalescence and abalone.
It was so musical it almost was a song,
I hummed along with what I thought I was hearing
until I became one with the paper and it was so good.
I wanted to stay there forever, but alas
some ignorant imbecile pressed "print"
and I exited the paper pixelated confetti dream
to move on to the 3rd and final immersion.

Scissors.
They were laying innocently on the windowsill.
Shimmering blindingly in a shaft of bolted sunlight.
They looked so inviting and yet so dangerous too.
I thought about the time when I was 4 years old,
sitting on the kitchen table playing with scissors,
pushing them gently into the fabric weave of my jeans;
upper thigh area. Not even considering they were dangerous.

My mother was at the sink. Turned. Saw what I was doing.
Said, in an imploring voice, "Be careful. Put them down.
They could slip and you could cut your leg."
I wondered what that would feel like,
so I pushed a bit harder each time I pushed.
Then the scissors thrust though the jeans into my leg
and the blood burst out through the jeans onto the denim.
My mother panicked, upset and flustered, but that passed.
Looking back it seems to me she was always a nervous wreck.
I wonder now if she was that way before I was born.

Perhaps so, but probably not.

This was just one of the many frights I gave her.
Anyhow the lesson learned was this.
Scissors are not dangerous. I am.

After the 3 immersions, what happens is this:

You realize Rocks have sentience and eyes
and they're spying on us as are other inanimate things.
Lesson learned: Don't trust anything. All is alive.

You realize white Paper is not white at all, it's technicolor.
Black paper is not black at all, it's 17 shades of white.
The world is a master of disguises in holographic spin.
Lesson learned: Nothing is as it seems.

You realize Scissors are shiny, and slick, sharp and useful,
possibly perilous and life-threatening.
Lesson learned: Scissors are not dangerous. People are.

In the final analysis, what happens is this.
You learn your lessons,
then you repeat your mistakes.

On Becoming Ricky Nelson

I started to follow the path in a lot of different directions.
All at once. What a trip. So good.
And that's fine at first, bee's knees and the whole nine
until it got too confusing and terrorizing.

Then something else started to stoke up.
It felt like "warmly funny" feels in the winter months.
So I started to follow the path in one direction at a time.
All at once. What a trip So much better.
And that was also fine at first, buzzing with excitement.
Then, through trial and error, I picked up peas and pods.
I even picked up peas in a pod and a world of pods in a pea.
I had the realization that edamame soybean pods
are, possibly, the best snack ever. Seriously.
What was I to do? Pretend I didn't have the realization.
Nah. I've always been a stick-hard, steely-eyed realist.
No lying for me. I am the truthsayer of the soothsayers.

So all at once I decided to become all of my selves
and let them all chat amongst themselves.
I kept one self out of the group, so I could attach myself to it
and eavesdrop on all my other selves to size them up.
See if they were good guys or outlaws. healers or killers.
During my many hours of eavesdropping
I came upon my super perfect self.
A spiritual, empath killer. I baptized it Spiremki.
I coddled it and brainwashed it just enough to bend it to my will.
Long story short. It killed all the other selves:
the good, the bad and the ugly and was the only self left.
Outside myself. It fact it really was myself,
but a much better self than the current myself,
so I coaxed Spiremki into killing the part of me that's me
and taking over so I could please everyone,
And, if I couldn't please everyone, then I'd have the courage
to change my name to Ricky Nelson,
attend garden parties ... and simply please myself.

Degrees

Sometimes you lose it before you can even get it on paper.
Or type it down. It fades in staccato degrees.
And those were the notions
bound to be the path to the Golden Line.
That's what poets seek. Endlessly.
The golden line that keeps slipping away in hazy degrees.

Yeah. The Golden Line.
Like a finding a white whale in the literary sea.
You'll know it if you read it.
But man oh man...when you write one!
Lord of mercy, it's more than bliss.
It's super bliss in that pure, raw and uncut form.

Writing poetry on the edges of the racing form
I need some diving intervention for a Golden Line
and for a winning horse today.
Sometimes you can stand so close
but still be just one degree removed.
Apart from the mirage of predetermined outcomes.
Like you're on the outside of the betting window
just sweating it out hard and agitated.
Not sure where to place the money. The long shot?
The sure thing (which rarely is)? The trifecta?

Then like manna from heaven you see it.
Number 6 "Degrees". Now that must be divine intervention.
The little voice inside your head keeps saying.
'It's a sign. Bet on it boy.'
So you sidle up to the betting window
already feeling like a sure-fire winner.
"$500 on number 6 in the 6th to win"
And a few minutes later you are one lucky s.o.b.
Degrees didn't win by a head.
Not even by a nose.
He won by... degrees.

Him Not Hem

I went to bed icy and tired.
I woke up in the pages of a Hemingway book.
It felt like a moveable feast.
But I can't be certain of that.
That's not what's important.
What's important is that I was refusing everything
I was being told to do by the director.
who was directing the dream.
By him, not by Hem.
By the director
And I had this feeling in the dream
that felt like it does when I'm awake
and the drink takes over.
Yes, it's pleasant.

Mebbee that's why I kept telling the director to screw off.
Lowered inhibitions and all that.
Anyway, in the dream I was drinking a beer
and the director told me drinking wasn't allowed on set.
So I emptied the can and looked him square in his soul.
Didn't say anything. Just did a squinty
"why can't I get this thing into focus" kind of look.

And once my vision cleared up,
I could see he was not any better than the rest.
The director that is.
Him, not Hem.

A – maze – ing

It's just another day's work.
We shove through.
We make it somehow.
Have you ever met a person who doesn't seem to work.
Claims to be an artist of some kind.
A creator of importance.
But never created anything important.
How do they pay rent?
That's always been my question.
Free rent?
Mommy owns the apartment?
Daddy owns the condo?
Mommy and daddy own the house?

Wow, that sounded jaded.
But sometimes the teeth become loosened
and the floss falls away.

Can you blame me?
I've been working since the age of 14.
Wow, that sounded self-righteous.

But sometimes the high horse seems so inviting.
After all, you can't sculpt a work of art with a hammer.
Wait, can you?
I think the key is the hammer can't ever be swung in anger.
But then again maybe sometimes it needs to be.

What a labyrinth of the mind.
a – MAZE – ing.
Jaded, self-righteous, hammered and angry.
I think I feel a poem coming on.

The Search Never Ends

I got back to Calgary after a grueling trip
through miles of dusty swayback switchbacks.
At the time I was living in a small little closet sized apartment
above a bar. I know…perfect, right?
So I got back with the intention of simply writing her a note
saying I was leaving and leaving it on the kitchenette table.

But I felt the bottles behind the bar making a play for me.
So I figured it would only be right to play with a couple.
But I swear, my intention was to have 2 quick cocktails,
write the note and stampede to the Stampede.
I bet you think you know where this is going. Don't you?

The letter was tougher than I thought it would be to write.
Not because I was all overcome with emotions
and finding it hard to take it easy on myself. No.
I just couldn't find a goddamn writing implement.
No pen, no pencil, no quill, no inkwell.
And we were always such fastidious stashers
of the tools of our craft. The oars for our raft of pages.
So I started flipping couch cushions, molesting the couch frame,
and ransacking the whole place.
Turning everything upside-down.
All this over because of having a woman but not having a pen.

In that moment I doubled over in irony.
And while I was doubled over I noticed my pants had no crease.
I mean I was going to the stampede in dress slacks with no crease.
It doesn't get any cheesier or sloppier than that,
I started asking around if anybody had an iron
and ironically the face behind the bottles smiled
and whispered 'nobody's gonna notice big boy'.
Being a bit booze-lazy at this point in time
I looked the bottle square in the eyes
and sincerely said 'Good advice Buds. Sage!

So I forgot about writing the note,
and I forgot about looking for an iron,
and I started to wonder why I used the word "Sage".
Then it hit me like a ton of old cow-patties turned brick.
I was in Calgary matey, and thar be sagebrushes there.
I looked out the window to confirm my revelation.
And yes ... one of 'em was there, just sitting and staring,
like a crackerjack, private eye, Sleepy Joe detective
trying to look presidential and secretly surveil me.
And then I mulled over the word "sagebrush",
broke it into two parts and lassoed the 'brush'.

I looked above and between the bottles on the bar
and peered into the mirror to check out my hair.
It looked a little unkempt, for a brush-cut,
and what is the inference as to what a brush-cut needs?
Of course. A brush!
So I forgot about writing the note,
I forgot about looking for an iron,
I forgot about the now separated sagebrush
and I began my search for the brush that ran away from the sage.
I couldn't find that vixen of a brush, but I kept searching.

I hot-footed it to the Stampede
and as soon as I paid my entrance fee and got through the gate
a scruffy bearded Bozo came up to me. Got in my face.
'Wanna buy a brush man? Looks like you could use one.'
Then he looked me over quickly and said
'There's a guy over there selling irons.
Looks like you could use one of them too.'

I felt like bopping him one,
but I just looked at him and smiled,
"Have you got a pen buddy? I really need a pen."
And in that penultimate moment I realized
the search never ends.

Random Moon Boy

Thoughts that may seem random to some
are not necessarily random to me.
Take the word 'random' and switch the 3rd and 6th letters.
The word becomes 'ramdon'. Now split the 2 syllables.
"Ram" "Don". But we can't do that or we'd be guilty of a felony.
Or we could split the split differently to "Ramd" "On"
And that would conjure up a couple of images:
An LA Ram running as he Ramd On to a Touchdown.
Or a Red Neck Dodge Ram driver on an obstacle course
Pulling wheelies, popping clutches as he Ramd On to winning.

Wandering on randomly and wondering, I have to ask:
Is it just me or are blue lights more calming than yellow lights?
To me it feels like they offer more accessibility to the iris.
And on the same bent, are eye jokes too cornea?
Or are they just astigmatisms being sarcastic.
Also wondering if eyeballs are easier to roll down hotdog alley?
Or if ten-pin bowling balls cut the mustard better.

Is it better to be particular or hardly selective at all?
When picking a winner at the track….being particular.
When picking your nose … hardly selective at all
When picking someone's brain … neither … just go for it.
Particular – you're likely to get what you want
Hardly selective - you'll likely have more memorable moments.
This is a tough one for some, but not for me.

I'm a believer in fate, karma, ordination. Call it what you may.
I just go for the gusto. Jump in the deepest part of the water
And spin the random wheel of luck and kiss my dice:
A true optimist spitting into the wind
in the most particular of random ways.

Some slackers call me Ramdon Boon Moy
Most call me Random Moon Boy
But that's just me. The yin and yang of me.
Boondoggle Boggle in the Boondocks

I kept my eyes on the floor in front of me the best I could.
And I allowed my thoughts to become still.
And a question came to me.
But before I could answer that question
another question boggled my brain waves.
Who is it that's asking the question?
Fair enough I thought. I felt boondoggled.

Somebody once told me if you see a monk sleeping
or slouching you have two choices.
Make him aware of it or let him continue on.
I thought that was fair enough as well.
I've caught myself nodding off in a similar way.
Like I was almost fully into now.

So I fell asleep and was transported
to a very remote destination in the Ozarks.
It was a village called Boondocks Bandaid 7
which was just Southeast of Crashburn 8.
and Due West of Serendipity 9.
They were all remote down in the Boondocks,
but only Bandaid was prefaced with Boondocks.
It was the largest of the villages and had the fewest buses
even fewer cars and motorcyles and a handful of tricycles,
but it was rich in horseflesh and cowhide
And blood and guts and broken tractor saddles.

The dirt road sign read 'Entering Bandaid 7'.
Came to it via Crashburn 8 and Serendipity 9.
On the dusty and bumpy go-nowhere main street
a grand mal boondoggle of hustlers were gathering.
They had lobe-scarred ears and razored pool cues.
These hustlers were cruisin' for a gang war.
The Bluebottles and the Flyswatters hated each other.
They always played to a tie in billiards tournaments
and both gangs were fed up with never winning.
The bookies, with beady eyes, sweaty foreheads
itchy palms and stogie-stuffed mouths,
were there setting odds and taking bets.
There wasn't much of a spread,

but still, the Swatters were the favourites
and the money and honey
were flowin' hard, fast and furious...
a sign of what was to come soon enough.

The tournament started off pleasant enough
until a Swatter swung around and clipped a Bluebottle
right in the middle of his left-winged arm.
The Bluebottle spun wildly in spirals, buzzing noisily,
then hit the ground like a turd from a tall cow's ass.

Then the fight was on and the timid were gone.
The oversized Swatters enlisted their daughters.
The Bluebottle tall ones enlisted their sons.
Lust was a must and the bookie went bust.
The Bottles and Swatters talked dowries and totters.
Took their Harleys from the stalls, went to Niagara Falls
Soon to be in-laws when the 7th crow calls.

Everyone in the Boondocks was thrilled ... almost to death,
that there would be no more boondoggles in the Boondocks
to boggle their kin folk or bootlegger outlaws.

Now the Flyswatters and Bluebottles
are a cool glad-hand clan, 'Down in the Boondocks'.
and Billy Joe Royal is making a long overdue comeback.
His old hit record is on iTunes, CD Baby etc.
and he's singin' the happies all the way to the bank baby.
And he's got a new contract to record his new song:
'Boondoggle Boggle in the Boondocks.'
Who knew??

Psychosomatic Fallacies
(aka the Legend of Ern)

My greatest psychosomatic fallacy is
that my greatest asset, my imagination,
is always in a position of idiosyncratic risk
and stark reality's glaring hard-edged eye.
Now, I'm not sayin' I'm a grey matter whiz.
No, I've never been accused of cornering that market
but I do believe we all need to dig up and face-down
all our psychosomatic fallacies, not just the biggest offenders.

I'm not saying it's a good idea or a bad idea.
but I do think on some level it helps to be
hepped up and relaxed in synchronicity.
Hard to do but can be done with a little synaptic tweaking.

Alright, now imagine this psychosomatic fallacy of sorts.
It would be like if a cheetah were to instantly and mysteriously
take on the sloth-like qualities of Jabba the Hutt.
That's how I feel. Like Jabba fighting Shai-Hulud.
Stuck between a lead-footed full-throttle acceleration
and the pull of the parking brake straight up at the same time.
Close your eyes and imagine it. Then drift and dream.
Back to the past and into the future and back to the present.
The dream weaver of psychosomatic fallacies
is fast asleep so you can easily slip his noose
and be on the road to recover in a split-hair second.

When the current incarnation comes clean
the visions get deeper and deeper.
And you may find yourself saying things like
"Thus and hence"; "Thee and Ye" and "Lo"
or "It's all nearing the airs of sacrosanctity.,
That's how you'll know it's incarnation bleed through.
It's freeing and stifling all at once, but as you get used to it,
you will be able to blend and shape yourself to a tee.

I had a job that was BO-ring. B-O-R-I-N-G!

But when my incarnation was cleaned
I was able to write my books on the company's dime.
You know what I mean? We all shirk sometimes.
And when the incarnation is murky and cluttered
you owe all of you to the bank, or the company or whatever.
Tennessee Ernie Ford knew this every day of his life.
He loaded 16 tons for the company and 1 ounce for himself.
He owed his soul to the company store.
He flipped St. Peter off when he was called to the gate,
Said, "Don't call me now Pete, cause I'm stuck in a hole.
The company's a hold on my body and soul."

See, this was a psychosomatic fallacy Ern believed
and as long as he believed, he was stuck ...
stuck in an uncleaned incarnation and working in a mine
was doing nothing to help him cleanse his incarnation.
Then one night he had a dream of his dead Grandpappy.
Gramps said "Wake up Ern. You fool, open your eyes.
You'll never see the forest for the trees, dummy,
until you light a match and move forward into them.
Well boy. What in tarnation are ya waitin' for.
Get out of the fart sack, march away from the mine
and into the lap of nature. Light the match.
Lift up your head and hands and pray for a cleansing.

So, long story short, Ern did what his Grandpappy said.
Then soon after, he heard St. Pete call again and this time
his incarnation was clean and sweet smelling
with the aroma of a thousand red carnations.
He ascended to the golden gates and entered.
His Grandpappy was there with St. Peter,
just a -ginnin' ear to ear waiting for him.
Gramps grabbed him by the shoulders and bear-hugged him,
saying "Ya did good fool. Ya listened to my words,
fer once in yer cockamamie life,
and finally left them goofy uncleaned mortal fools down there.
And ya left 'em with a moral and a story to think on.
It'll go somethin' like this:
When your heart feels as heavy as 16 tons,
remember it well 'The Legend of Ern'

and head on out to the forest for sustenance.
Light a match and burn up all them Gol'durned
psychosomatic fallacies and start to live.
I mean really live sans psychosomatic fallacies,
and give thanks in the name of Tennessee Ernie Ford
that inarticulate and inadvertent spreader
of these immortal powerful words in the hymn,
written to help unclean incarnates find their way.
'Burnin' up the Fallacies:

Burn them fallacies; and get on the good foot
and lose 16 tons in 30 days!
Order today for a limited time bonus offer,
and get a lifetime supply of free spirit shake-ups
when you order the new miracle diet ...
The Erni-System – weight loss for the cleansing incarnates.
Order today and we'll also send you
our special 'wipe away psychosomatic fallacies' cream,
GUARANTEED to wipe them out completely.
AND ... wait for it ... a ticket to the promise land too!

Hallelujah to all the incarnates. Bless 'em all!
the cleansed and uncleansed; the static and in progress;
the lost and the found; the good, the bad and the ugly
and, if he ever cleans up his bad-ass act,
— Ern's once upon a time hero —.
That's right ... Dirty Harry!
Bless his sorry ass too.

Finicky Widget

A moral compass is such a finicky widget.
and I think my gauge has always read
a bit looser than others.
One day I decided to open the darn thing up.
Tinker around with it a bit.

First thing I noticed when I cracked it open
was how wonky the inner workings looked.
And then to my utter shock and surprise,
there was this tiny little man
sitting in a tiny little rocking chair,
smoking a rather large pipe
(relative to his small stature).
I asked him who he was
and what he was doing
inside of my moral compass.
Said he was screwing it up.

I must have caught him off guard
as he started fumbling around with the tobacco for his pipe
which he had been sitting on apparently,
because he just kept rolling his butt cheeks left and right
and pulling tobacco leaves out from under the cushion
of his dilapidated noisily creaking
very ancient rocking chair.

I took out my mind magnifying glass for a closer look.
Hmmm. looked like it could use a fresh coat of paint too,
over and above some cedar oil to quiet the creaks.

What was odd was that the tobacco leaves
were as big as he was and even bigger,
but maybe that wasn't that odd after all
because tobacco leaves can be pretty darn big.
Especially in his teensy-weensy world.

I used to love to drive through the Pioneer Valley

in Massachusetts just to visit the old tobacco farms.
They still hung the leaves to dry in the huge barns
and you could smell the sweet, dank aromas
from miles away if the wind was firing right on any given day.
But that's not what this poem is about
and I promise to lace for you
the most beautiful and romantic poem
about the tobacco barns of Massachusetts one day.
Just not today.

So, back to the little fella in my compass.
The creaks in his rocking chair got me to thinking about
another creak ... and John, Michelle, Cass and Denny
gettin' kind of itchy and workin' for a penny.
singin' and dancin' their days away in Creeque Alley.
Do you remember that one pallie? I do, and always with a sigh.

I was lost in thought for a few moments and then shocked back
by the booming voice coming from the tiny man in the rocking chair.
"Of course I remember that Random Moon Boy" he smirked.
"Bet you didn't know I knew your real name and who you are.
I have my methods and my watchers, so don't ever think I don't.
I remember it because John Phillips was my first born
and there were times I thought of him as my worst born.
Back in his rebellious weed smoking, cocaine sniffing days.
But, he got over that bad news and that was a good thing.

Anyhow, I wanted to let you know we're not all failed singers
or rabble-rousing wanna-be down in the mouth poets.
My father, Johnny Thompson invented the Phillips screwdriver
and then changed his surname to Phillips. Why you ask?
He was sick and tired of being nicknamed 'Tommie Boy".

I told the tiny guy I enjoyed his stories and would visit again
if he would try to fix the gauge inside my moral compass.
He said he'd put it at the top of his priority list.
We both hoisted an imaginary pint and cheered each other.

I went back to my normal life and felt a weight had been lifted.
I didn't have to worry about my moral compass anymore.

It was being looked after by a tiny old guy in a rocking chair
who was a blood relative of some super talented dudes
One of the Papas of the Mamas and Papas
and the revered although still somewhat unknown
inventor of the Phillips screwdriver which, by the way,
was the driver the tiny guy was using to get a screw in one
on the heavy metal golf course of my moral compass.

Yes ... a moral compass is such a finicky widget
and a broken one is a real winicky fidget.
I never worry at night, though, because every night
is a re-run of the Tonight Show and the old familiar intonations
of Ed McMahon's voice announcing ... Here's Johnny ...
and I know the moral compass daily maintenance
is only a tick-tocking, northeasterly heartbeat away.

One Moment to Another

I've been luckier than I deserve in life
and lived it the only way I've known how.
Now that that's out of the way...
let's get into it if you're still interested.
There are moments and then ... there are moments,
and they never deviate or levitate, they just meditate
and medicate and chase one moment to another.

I always believed in an admixture of well-planned,
off the cuff, and hardly a thought given beforehand.
I've also always believed in allowing it to be
as near as a stone's throw it that feels right.
One of the first lessons my sensei taught me
was to retire from the struggle and simply write instead.
She also taught me a few different ways to be at one
with feeling, like natural landscapes are.
I'll never forget this one time when she asked me
if I had ever gone through a phase where
I was drawn out each evening to stare at the moon.
I said I had. Said the moon was my sibling in silence.
Said some folks call me Moon Boy as I'm never static.
I'm either waxing or waning, and sometimes I wax-wane.
I asked sensei the significance of staring at the moon.
She said there wasn't any significance to it whatsoever.
Only the moment after the one we are in is significant.

Alright let's switch from one moment to another.
There's not really as much enjoyment to be found
in the pseudo-stuff. Would you agree?
That's probably why, for me, the road always led back to writing.
It has a magnetic hold the other things just don't.
It's my grey matter formed into letters and then into words
and then spilled like finely aged wine onto paper,
and its beautiful noises rising in my throat,
caressing my tongue, coming out of my mouth
one moment to another ad infinitum.

Waiting

The strangest things happen when your sitting there
waiting for the inspiration to strike. You think things like...
"You don't need a big following, you need a strong following."
"The 178 rejection slips, letters, emails and voicemails
from the publishers were a good thing."
"Maybe my chakra system is askew."
Yeah, you really think those things. Inexhaustibly.
Then it happens. And you forget all that real quick.
Like it never happened.
Because you're too busy riding a wave.
And you're rising into fame and out of failure.
And that's powerful. That moment is so powerful.

But that too is fleeting. Everything is.
And that's a good thing. It couldn't happen otherwise.
So you resolve to accept the good with the bad
and the ups with the downs. And that feels fine.
Fits nicely like a hard-stone sensibility.
Fits perfectly like a tongue and groove papyrus leaf.
And there's plenty of those in some other realm.
So when it fleets it rebuilds at the same time.
Oh wait ... where were we? Did I go off on a tangent?

Ok, so yeah, when you're sitting there
waiting for the inspiration to strike...
run the gate, ride the bull and break the horse.
Grab inspiration from the heart of its dream.
Strike the match, light up a smoke, light up your life
and burn the flames of inspiration into the wood,
carving the poem into the dark of its age
so it can be reborn again into the glory of the words.
The words now dripping and drooling from your pen
onto the stage of the waiting world.
Some say the world is waiting for a sunrise.
I say it's waiting for inspiration ... waiting for a poem.

Fruit of the Fodder

Trodding the earth with a purposeful gait
I try to do at least one thing for my craft each day.
Even if that something is assembling and disassembling
my Russian nesting dolls for an hour.
Or eating pickles and green beans before bedtime.
Or frying bannock Coho, pickled beets and chocolate syrup
for a nice light Sumo recommended midnight snack.
How on earth could that help with the writing process?
Is that what you were going to ask?
Well, I'll tell you.

The nesting dolls serve to fondle the brain toggle a bit.
And the pickles and green beans,
for some bizarre reason unbeknownst to me,
cause me to experience vivid and wildly insane dreams.
And the dreams in turn serve as food for my poetic fodder.
The bannock, Coho, pickled beets and chocolate
are a slap in the gut wake up call to get movin'
and groove the last bit of pulp out of the paper.
Make it pristine for my virgin words of ink
to penetrate the beckoning soft flesh of the white.

Ready for poetry and loaded for bear with my cap-gun
I put on my crepe paper slippers, miniaturize myself
and sprint up and down my blank, pre-poem paper.
This creates a nice haphazard grid weave of tree slice.
Then I take off my slippers and carry my mind, barefoot,
across the weave of the blank pre-poem page.
And oh the sweet poetic rain that falls on my brainwaves
mixing and melding and producing a gaggle of words
to excite and tingle-tangle-tongle the vowels and consonants
into a symphonic-rock'n'roll-grungey immortal classic.

The poem hops, skips, jumps, dances frantically
and twirls itself from the pulsating womb of my mind
into a myriad of shapes, sounds, visions and emotions
that cling to each other descending the birth channel

awaiting the final tidal wave push to the finish.
To brilliantly glimmer and gleam, shine and sparkle
beneath the operating room fluorescent overhead lights.

With every line I write I watch the tsunami build
alive with soft and tender words that soothe
and screaming and wailing words that excite.
They mumble and tumble through the waters of my soul.
And as the wave reaches shoreline of poetic promise,
the fruit of the fodder is born ...
the living breathing poem,
patiently awaiting its name.

Signals

It's not always a signal from the great beyond.
If only it was that simple.
Sometimes you have to strip it
right down to the bone.
And use the gifts that you've been given.
And you've got to stay up on things.
When you do these things
even "more of the same" can change your views.
That mixed with other things.
But it's really all hinged on the ability
to channel that thing that never leaves.

There are signs of never slowing
and there are signs of decay all around us.
All matter matters.
That's a movement that should catch a bit of tread
circa 3021.
That's my guess.
If you feel that then you are ahead of your time as well.

On a completely other trajectory and note,
the music sounds so majestic tonight.
But maybe that's not so much beside the point after all.
Did you know the beat of a drum
is one of the oldest sounds
a human type could ever replicate?
I didn't either. Until I did,
then the narrative changed.

I wish safe traveling upon you all.
I really do.
I wish literary awakenings upon you all.
I really do.
I wish there was no time limit to the whole thing.
But don't we all?

But really, maybe there is no time limit at all,
Maybe we are in a continuous loop of the same incarnation
over and over again with a slight cleanse between incarnations
so we hardly remember anything, if anything,
from the previous exact incarnation
in exactly the same time period and location
with the same relatives and opportunities.
Maybe we just have to keep doing it over and over
until we get it right, like a painting, or a poem,
Actually we are all paintings and poems
dripping from the universal brush
onto our own individual canvas and paper.

And maybe déjà vu is just a quick flashback
to ourselves in the same life as before, again and again.

I know I've stood in the kitchen and looked at my mother:
and she was pouring the same cup of coffee into the same cup
and she was dressed in the same clothes as before
and I knew. I knew exactly what she was going to say,
And it was something totally unrelated to the conversation,
to the moment, to the time, to the feeling.
And then she said exactly what I knew she would say.
Word for word...EXACTLY!

Something like that.
Well ... something like that is a signal
from the dimension beyond.
Where they, whoever they is,
on the other side of the one-way mirror can see us
but we can't see them.

Well ... that is a signal, my friend.
That is a signal.

Signals, signals, signals.
I should have joined the signal corps.
when I had the chance.

Authors Profile

Jose & James are a rough and tumble, sensitive collaborative team, living off-planet. They are seekers and gatherers of obscure thoughts and bizarre moments in the quantum boiling pot of timeless time. When they are not writing poetry, their hobby is chasing nuclear butterflies with their collapsible net of poetry as they time travel through their air stream of ink and words, polishing their poems to a super-fine gloss and shine.

If you watch closely you may be able to see them flashing in and out of time on retrograde Moon rotational nights.

Mebbee ... Mebbee not.

www.ingramcontent.com/pod-product-compliance
Lightning Source LLC
Chambersburg PA
CBHW062146100526
44589CB00014B/1702